TRANSPORTATION

DAVID GLOVER

World Book

in association with
TWOCAN

How to use this book

Contents
The contents page at the front of the book lists the main subjects in the book and tells you their page number.

Cross-references
Above the heading on the page, you will find a list of subjects that are related to the topic. These subjects are listed with their page numbers. Turn to these pages to find out more about each subject.

Glossary words
Difficult words are explained in the glossary on page 46. In the Book, these words are written in bold.

Index
The index is on pages 47–48. It is a list, in alphabetical order, of important words used in the book. The page numbers are written next to the words. If you want to read about a subject, look it up in the index, then turn to the page number given.

Titles in this series
Animals
Atlas
Earth
Space
Transportation

Published in the United States by
World Book, Inc., 233 N. Michigan Avenue,
Suite 2000, Chicago, IL 60601
in association with Two-Can Publishing

Art director: Belinda Webster
Managing editor: Deborah Kespert
Senior designer: Helen Holmes
Commissioning editor: Julia Hillyard
Editorial support: Flavia Bertolini, Amanda Nathan, Robert Sved
Picture research: Laura Cartwright
Consultant: John Becklake
Main illustrations: Nick Hawken
Computer illustrations: Mel Pickering
U.S. editor: Sharon Nowakowski

**For information on other World Book products, call 1-800-WORLDBK (967-5325),
or visit our Web site at http://www.worldbook.com**

Library of Congress Cataloging-in-Publication Data
Glover, David, 1953 Sept. 4-
    Transportation/David Glover.
    p.   cm. — (Picture reference)
    Includes index.
    Summary: Introduces the various ways by which people travel
    including cycles and skates, cars, trucks, emergency vehicles,
    trains, boats, and helicopters
    ISBN 0-7166-9906-0 (hc) — ISBN 0-7166-9907-9 (sc)
    1. Transportation–Juvenile literature. [1. Transportation.]
I. Title. II. Series: Picture reference (Chicago, Ill.)
TA1149.G57 1998   98-3378
629.04-dc21

Photographic credits:
B & C Alexander p42, p43br; Britstock-IFA/Bernd Ducke p5, p13, p16, B-IFA p17tl; Image Bank/Leo Mason p9, IB/Paolo Curto p19tl, IB/Andy Caulfield p20, IB/Guido A. Rossi p35tl; James Davis Travel Photography p12; Japan Marine Science & Technology Center p33; NASA/Science Photo Library p35br; Pictor International p15, p25c; Pictures Colour Library p27; Powerstock Photo Library/A Gin p7br, p25t; Quadrant Picture Library/Anthony R. Dalton p17br; Rick Tomlinson p19c; Robert Harding Picture Library/Christopher Rennie p24, RHPL/Ron Behrmann p34; Tony Stone Images/Lori Adamski Peek p7tl, TSI/Mark Joseph p11, TSI/Paul Chesley p23, TSI p28, TSI/James Balog p29, TSI/Mike Sarowiak p37, TSI/Arnulf Husmo p39, TSI/David R Frazier p43t.

Printed in Spain

(hc) 2 3 4 5 6 7 8 9 10 02 01 00

Contents

How do people travel?

For thousands of years, the only way we could travel from one place to another was by walking or by riding animals. Since then, we have discovered faster ways of moving around. Bicycles, cars, buses, and trains carry us over land, while ships take us across the oceans. We also fly through the air in huge airplanes, and we can even travel into space and back.

▶ Camels are perfect for carrying people and goods long distances across hot deserts. Camels have wide feet that do not sink into the sand.

Changing transport
This timeline shows important inventions that have changed the way people travel.

Wheel	Sailboat	Hot-air balloon	Steam train
about 3500 B.C.	about 3000 B.C.	1783	1825

Nobody knows who invented the wheel, but an ancient people called the Sumerians were the first people to attach wheels to carts pulled by oxen.

The ancient Egyptians were the first people to use sailboats. They made them from planks of wood and added linen sails to drive them across the water.

People were first carried into the air by hot-air balloons. Two French brothers, Joseph and Jacques Montgolfier, built the first successful hot-air balloon.

An Englishman called George Stephenson designed the first train to carry passengers. It was driven by steam and had a top speed of 15 mi. (24 km) per hour.

▶ **City** streets are often packed with cars, buses, vans, and other **vehicles**. Too many vehicles cause noise, traffic jams, and **pollution**.

Motorcar 1885	Airplane 1903	Space rocket 1961	Space shuttle 1981

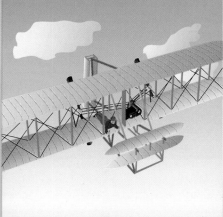

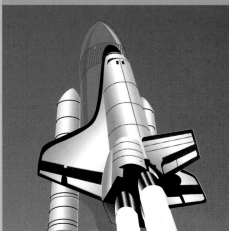

A German called Karl Benz built the first motorcar. It looked like a three-wheeled bicycle, but it was powered by an **engine** that burned **gasoline**.

The Americans Wilbur and Orville Wright built the first successful airplane, *The Flyer*. On its first flight, it flew just 120 ft. (37 m) and was in the air for 12 seconds.

In 1961, a Russian space rocket sent the first person into space. In 1969, two U.S. astronauts landed on the moon. They traveled in the rocket shown above.

Space shuttles were the first **spacecraft** that could be reused. On board, a crew of **astronauts** carries out repairs and experiments in space.

Cycles and skates

Cycles and skates are **vehicles** with wheels that you power with your legs. They cost very little to run and repair, and they do not have **engines** that **pollute** the air. In 1839, in Scotland, the first two-wheeled cycle with pedals was built. It was called a bicycle. Today, all over the world, millions of people ride bicycles. Cycling is faster than walking, and it keeps people fit and healthy.

helmet
The rider wears a helmet to protect his head.

Bicycle
This boy is riding a mountain bike. It has a tough **steel** frame and chunky tires for cycling over rough land. As the boy rides, he uses his leg **muscles** to push the pedals around. This moves a chain that turns the back wheel.

tire
Inside the thick rubber tire, there is a tube pumped full of air.

gears
This bicycle has several **gears**. Changing to a lower gear makes it easier to cycle uphill.

chain

pedal

handlebars
The rider controls the brakes and gears from the handlebars. The handlebars also help steer the bicycle.

brakes
When the rider brakes, these brake pads rub against the wheels and stop the bicycle.

Rollerblades

Traveling on rollerblades is great fun and good exercise. You can practice tricks in the park or skate past pedestrians on your way home. Skaters wear knee and elbow pads, gloves, and crash helmets to protect their bodies if they fall.

Racing bike

A lightweight racing bike zooms along at high speed. It has smooth narrow tires that roll easily along the road. The rider holds onto special upright grips on her handlebars and leans forward into the wind. A **streamlined** helmet and tight clothing help her to cut smoothly through the rushing air.

Skateboarding

A skateboard has four roller-skate wheels attached to a board. You need good balance to stand on the board and glide along. Skateboarders practice on special tracks. Expert skateboarders can leap, twist, and even somersault without falling.

Rickshaw

This three-wheeled cycle is called a rickshaw. In many Asian countries, passengers pay rickshaw drivers to take them across town. It is hard work for the driver, particularly in hot weather. Rickshaws are popular in crowded cities because they provide low-cost transportation, and they can squeeze through traffic jams.

Go to Cycles and skates page 6

Motorcycle

A motorcycle has two wheels and an **engine** attached to a strong frame. Traveling by motorcycle is a fast and easy way to move around. A rider can dart through traffic jams and squeeze into small parking spaces. Riding a motorcycle is exciting and fun but, to be safe, riders must wear sturdy leather clothes and a helmet. These help keep them warm and dry as they speed along and protect them if they fall.

windshield
The windshield helps to make the motorcycle more **streamlined** by pushing rushing air over the top of the rider.

Trail bike
A trail bike is built for riding off the road. It can travel along country trails, climb hills, and even cross streams. It has thick tires for extra grip.

headlight
A bright headlight tells others that the motorcycle is coming and at night, it lets the rider see the road ahead.

Motor scooter
A motor scooter is perfect for riding in cities. It has small wheels and a comfortable platform for the rider's feet. It is cheaper and easier to ride than a full-sized motorcycle.

treads
In wet weather, grooves in the tires, called treads, push away rain water. This helps to keep the motorcycle from skidding.

rear-view mirror
Before passing another vehicle, the rider checks her rear-view mirror to see if there are any **vehicles** behind.

Motorcycle racing
Motorcycle racing is a thrilling, but risky sport. To balance their bikes around turns, the riders lean over until their knees almost touch the ground.

fuel tank
Gasoline is stored in the **fuel** tank. To fill the tank, the rider unscrews a cap and pours in the gas.

pannier
Containers called panniers are useful for carrying tools and extra clothes.

Factfile

The world's smallest working motorcycle is about 4 in. (10 cm) high and 6 in. (15 cm) long. It is so small that it can stand on a saucer.

The first motorcycle was built in 1885 by Gottfried Daimler. It was made of wood with a gasoline engine.

In 1991, Yasuyuki Kudo rode on one wheel of his motorcycle for 224 mi. (331 km).

engine
An engine that burns **gasoline** powers the motorcycle.

gear lever
To change **gear**, the rider pushes the gear lever up or down with her foot.

Car

In many countries, the car is the most popular way of traveling. The first cars, built just over 100 years ago, were noisy and slow, and they often broke down. Modern cars are more reliable and much faster. They are designed to be comfortable for both long and short trips. But today, in many cities, there are so many cars that they create long traffic jams and **pollute** the air.

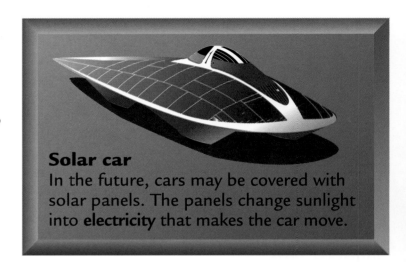

Solar car
In the future, cars may be covered with solar panels. The panels change sunlight into **electricity** that makes the car move.

steering wheel
The driver uses the steering wheel to turn the car's wheels left or right.

dashboard
Lights and dials on the dashboard show the car's speed and the amount of gas in the tank.

engine
The **engine** is usually at the front of the car, under the hood. The engine burns **gasoline** and makes the wheels move.

pedals
To go faster, the driver pushes the accelerator pedal. This sends more gas to the engine. The brake pedal slows down the car.

seat belt
The driver and passengers wear seat belts to protect them if they are in an accident.

brake
When the driver presses the brake pedal, pads inside the wheels push down to stop the car.

Factfile

There are over 300 million cars in the world. If you lined them up end to end, they would reach farther than the moon and back!

The world's longest car is a stretch limousine. It has 26 wheels, a swimming pool, and a double bed!

More Volkswagen Beetles have been built than any other car. There are over 20 million.

Built by robots
Cars are made up of hundreds of parts that are put together in a factory. Sparks fly as **robots** attach the parts to the body of each car. A new car is completed every few minutes.

trunk
There is space for luggage in the trunk at the back of the car.

turn signal
Flashing turn signals warn other people that the driver is going to turn or pull out.

tail pipe
Exhaust gases from the engine come out through a tail pipe.

Go to Emergency vehicles page 18, Road page 14, Traveling on snow page 42

Truck

A truck is a large **vehicle** that carries goods from place to place. It may take goods from one part of town to another or drive for days to another country. Trucks have powerful **engines**, which run on **diesel fuel**, to pull their heavy loads. Many trucks are built to do special tasks, such as move materials around a building site.

Driver's cab
On long trips, the cab is the driver's home. It is roomy and comfortable with a bed at the back for sleeping.

Articulated truck

Most large trucks are articulated, which means that they are made up of two parts that hook together. This allows the truck to turn corners more easily. The front section, called a tractor, has a powerful engine and a driver's cab. It hauls a long trailer loaded with goods.

tractor
The tractor easily unhooks so that it can pull different kinds of trailers.

trailer
This refrigerated trailer keeps fruit or meat fresh on the way to the supermarket.

Road train

A road train is a long truck that transports goods to places where there is no railroad. Its powerful engine pulls several heavy trailers over long distances. This road train is carrying two enormous tankfuls of **gasoline** all the way across Australia. Underneath, it has 42 wheels to support its heavy load.

Building roads

Modern trucks work together to build new roads as quickly as possible. Each truck has its own job and carries out the work of hundreds of people with shovels. Some trucks clear the ground, dig ditches, or carry away soil, while others deliver building materials, such as cement or pipes. Enormous tires help the trucks move over the rough ground.

ditch digger
A ditch digger has a long arm with sharp teeth for cutting out ditches. It moves on **caterpillar tracks.**

cement truck
Wet cement is mixed in the spinning drum of a cement truck. It pours out through a chute.

front-end loader
A front-end loader shovels up loose soil and carries it away in a large bucket.

Garbage truck
A garbage truck takes trash from outside your home to the garbage dump. A lift at the back of the truck picks up a garbage bin and empties it into the truck. Inside, a ram squashes the trash down. When the truck reaches the dump, the trailer tips up and the garbage tumbles out.

Fork-lift truck
Fork-lift trucks move heavy boxes and crates around a warehouse. The boxes rest in piles on flat pieces of wood called pallets. The driver just slides the truck's two long forks through a pallet and pushes a lever inside the cab to lift the boxes.

Go to Car page 10, Traveling on snow page 42, Truck page 12

Road

Long roads cut across most countries, linking towns and cities along the way. Roads make it easy for people to travel quickly from one place to another. The first roads were rough, muddy, and narrow but today, in most places, they are wider and smoother with sloping sides that let rain water drain away.

▶ Near cities, small roads link up with wide, high-speed roads called expressways.

expressway
On an expressway, cars often travel 55 mi. (88 km) per hour.

shoulder
In an emergency, drivers pull onto the shoulder to wait for help.

off-ramp
An off-ramp gives **vehicles** leaving the expressway plenty of room to slow down.

lane
An expressway has several lanes. Drivers use two of the lanes for passing slower vehicles.

Cats'-eyes are pieces of glass that line highway lanes and reflect a car's headlights. At night, they help drivers to see where they are going.

Signs help keep drivers safe. There are many different kinds, including signs that tell the speed limit.

Traffic lights control the traffic at intersections. Red tells drivers to stop, yellow shows that the lights are about to change, and green means go.

tunnel
It is much faster to drive through a tunnel than around or over a mountain.

bypass
Many vehicles avoid the busy city center by driving around it on a bypass.

overpass
An overpass is a road built above another road so that cars can pass quickly without stopping.

intersection
An intersection is where two or more roads meet. Drivers can turn on to another road at an intersection.

Getting across
A bridge is a quick way for traffic to cross rivers, valleys, and railroads. The Golden Gate Bridge in California is almost 2 mi. (3 km) long. It is held up by cables that loop down from towers.

Factfile

The longest traffic jam in history took place in 1980 outside Lyon, France. It was 109 mi. (176 km) long, which is equal to 44,000 cars standing bumper to bumper!

Spaghetti Junction in England is a famous tangle of roads that cross each other in one place. Eighteen roads meet on six different levels.

Go to Road page 14, Train page 20

Bus and streetcar

A bus carries many passengers at a time along set **routes**. It takes people on long trips as well as on short city trips. Many years ago, buses were pulled by horses, but today most buses have large **engines** that use **diesel fuel**. Streetcars are similar to buses, but they run on tracks through the city streets and are powered by **electricity**. Traveling by bus and streetcar saves **fuel** and reduces traffic on roads.

City bus
A ride on a modern city bus is quiet and smooth. Passengers buy their tickets in advance from the ticket office or a machine, or they pay on board. Along the route, large **automatic** doors slide open at bus stops so that people can step on and off.

Chugging along
This bright-red London bus is a double-decker. Passengers travel on two levels, called the upper and lower **decks**. On some buses, a conductor collects the fares while the driver sits in the cab, concentrating on the traffic.

bell
Passengers ring a bell to let the driver know they want to get off at the next stop.

bus station
The bus begins its journey at a bus station. People wait under shelters for their buses to arrive.

Crowded bus

In countries where there are few cars, the only way to travel may be by bus. This bus is packed with people taking their goods to market. When the bus is full inside, bags, buckets, and even animals are piled high on the roof.

School bus

Many children live too far from their school to walk back and forth so, on school days, they may travel to school on special buses. Flashing lights or signs warn other drivers to stop as the children step on and off.

destination plate
A destination plate with a name or a number shows where the bus is going.

Streetcar

Some towns and cities have streetcars as well as buses. Streetcars run on **steel** tracks set into city streets. A metal frame on the roof, called a pantograph, powers the streetcar by picking up electricity from overhead cables. Streetcars have been used since 1880, but when cars and buses became more common, many streetcar tracks were torn up to make wider roads. Recently, streetcars have become popular again, because they **pollute** the air less than buses do.

Go to Airport page 40, Ferry page 26, Helicopter page 38, Working boats page 28

Emergency vehicles

In an emergency, people need help quickly, so special **vehicles** speed to the rescue. Flashing lights and wailing sirens tell you that they are on their way. These vehicles are designed for different jobs and carry the latest equipment. The men and women who operate them are highly trained.

Fire engine

Fire engines carry huge ladders and long hoses to the scene of a fire. The ladder on the back of this fire engine can be lengthened to lift the firefighter high into the air, either to rescue a person or to shoot a powerful jet of water into the flames.

water supply
Water is pumped from a fire hydrant or from a tank in the fire engine.

platform
A firefighter stands on the platform at the top of the ladder to put out the flames.

turntable
The long ladder swivels into position on a revolving base called a turntable.

supporting jacks
The supporting jacks keep the fire engine level while the ladder is raised.

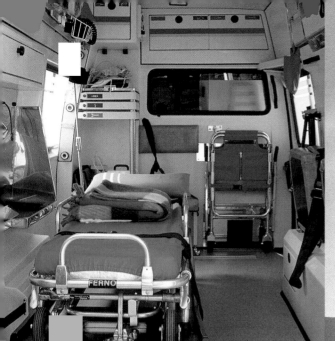

Police car

A police car is often the first vehicle to arrive at a traffic accident. Warning lights, sirens, and reflective stripes make sure that it can be seen easily by day or night. This police officer is using his car radio to call for other emergency services to bring more help.

Ambulance

When someone has an accident or suddenly becomes ill, an ambulance may take that person to the hospital. The ambulance has first-aid equipment so that trained medical workers can treat the patient immediately.

Lifeboat

A lifeboat rescues people in trouble at sea. It carries floats and lifebelts that the crew throws to people in the water to help them to safety. It also has medical and firefighting equipment on board. Although lifeboats are small, they are made of tough plastic that can survive the roughest seas. This modern lifeboat is self-righting, which means that if the boat turns over in a storm, it will flip the right way up again by itself.

Tow truck

When your car breaks down, you can use a telephone to call for a tow truck. If the truck driver cannot repair your car, he or she will attach it to the back of the truck and tow it to a garage. Tow trucks need to be sturdy to pull heavy vehicles and to work in bad weather.

Train

A train is a line of carriages pulled along a railroad track by a special car called a locomotive. Most locomotives are powered by **diesel fuel** or **electricity**. Trains carry passengers and goods quickly and safely between towns and cities. On many modern trains, passengers on long trips can eat in the dining car, make telephone calls, and even sleep overnight in a sleeping car.

All around the world
This powerful train uses diesel fuel to run its electric motors. Diesel-electric trains were first developed in the 1950's. Today, they are the most common types of trains in the world.

▼ This modern train is powered entirely by electricity. It shoots across the land at speeds of up to 186 mi. (300 km) per hour.

pantograph
An insulated framework called a pantograph carries electricity from overhead cables.

driver's cab
In the cab, the driver uses a radio to keep in touch with controllers in railroad stations along the way.

locomotive
The locomotive pulling this train is called a power car. It uses electricity fron the overhead cables to run the **motors**.

electric motor
Electric motors behind these springs turn the wheels.

20

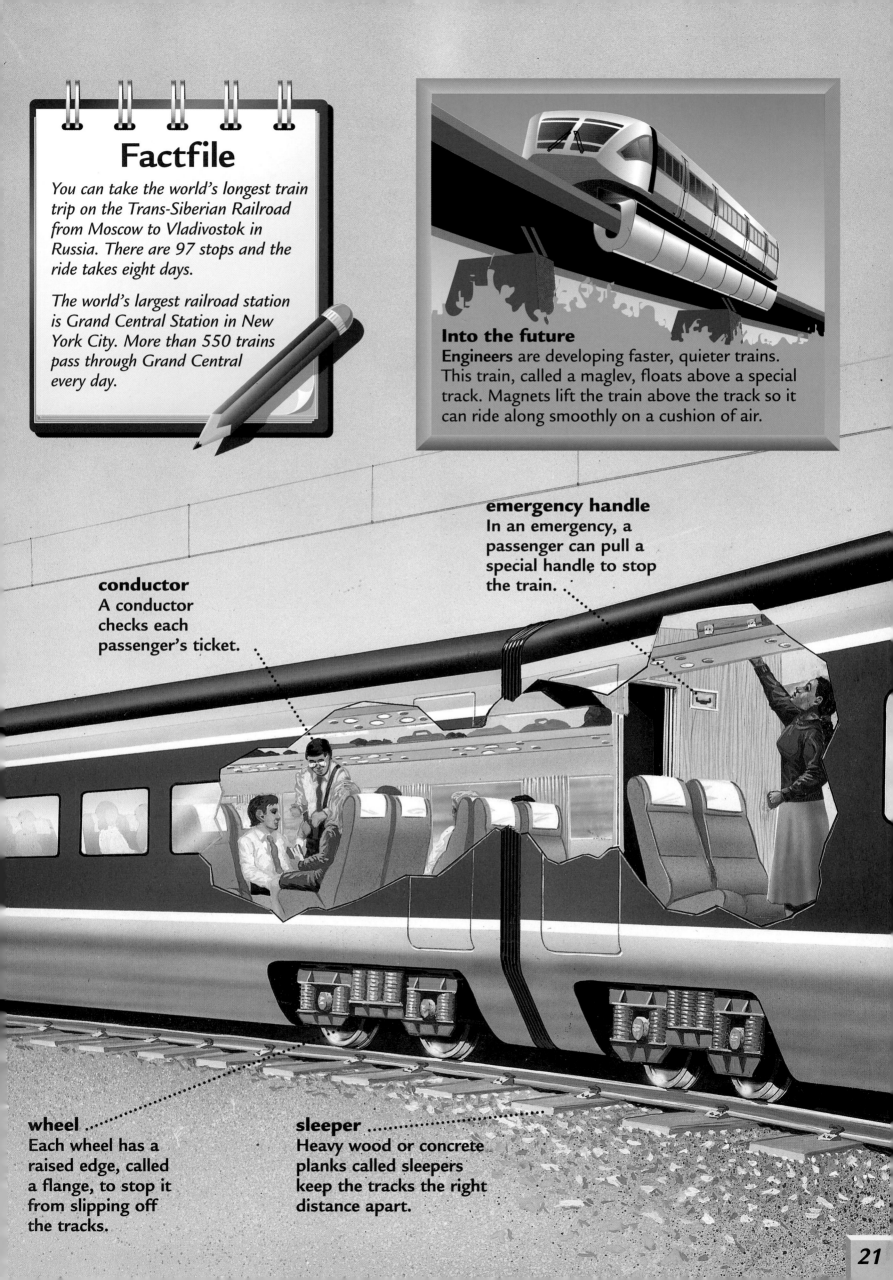

Factfile

You can take the world's longest train trip on the Trans-Siberian Railroad from Moscow to Vladivostok in Russia. There are 97 stops and the ride takes eight days.

The world's largest railroad station is Grand Central Station in New York City. More than 550 trains pass through Grand Central every day.

Into the future

Engineers are developing faster, quieter trains. This train, called a maglev, floats above a special track. Magnets lift the train above the track so it can ride along smoothly on a cushion of air.

emergency handle
In an emergency, a passenger can pull a special handle to stop the train.

conductor
A conductor checks each passenger's ticket.

wheel
Each wheel has a raised edge, called a flange, to stop it from slipping off the tracks.

sleeper
Heavy wood or concrete planks called sleepers keep the tracks the right distance apart.

Go to Train page 20

Subway train

Subway trains run through tunnels beneath city streets. Every day, in busy cities such as London, New York, and Paris, hundreds of thousands of people take the subway to go shopping or to travel to school or work. Entrances at street level lead passengers down to subway stations deep underground. Their trains arrive regularly, every few minutes.

▶ This picture shows the different levels of a subway station.

station entrance
Stairs lead down from the station entrance into the subway.

TICKETS

TICKETS

ticket machine
You buy your ticket from a machine or from a ticket agent.

barrier
An **automatic** barrier may check your ticket before letting you through.

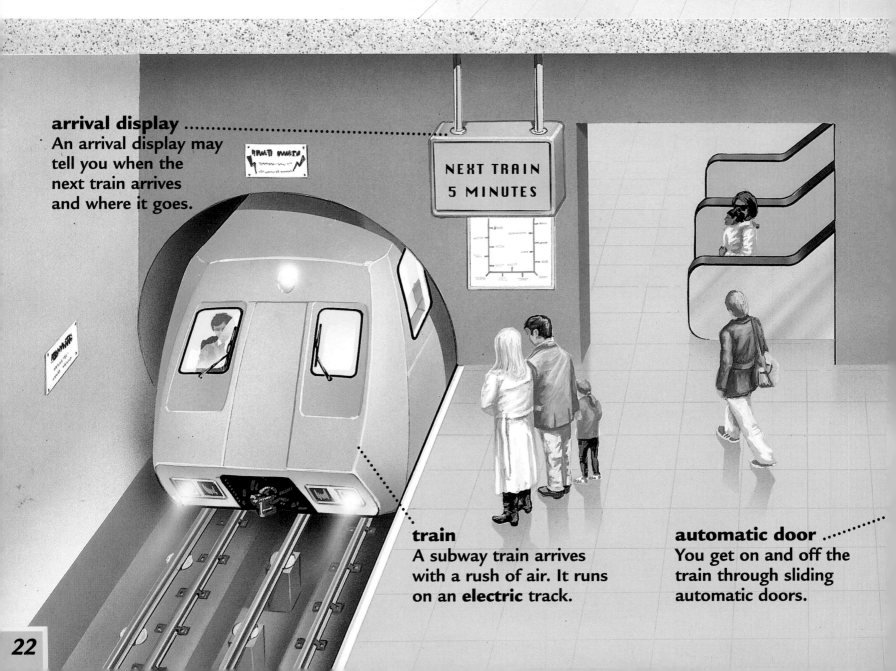

arrival display
An arrival display may tell you when the next train arrives and where it goes.

NEXT TRAIN
5 MINUTES

train
A subway train arrives with a rush of air. It runs on an **electric** track.

automatic door
You get on and off the train through sliding automatic doors.

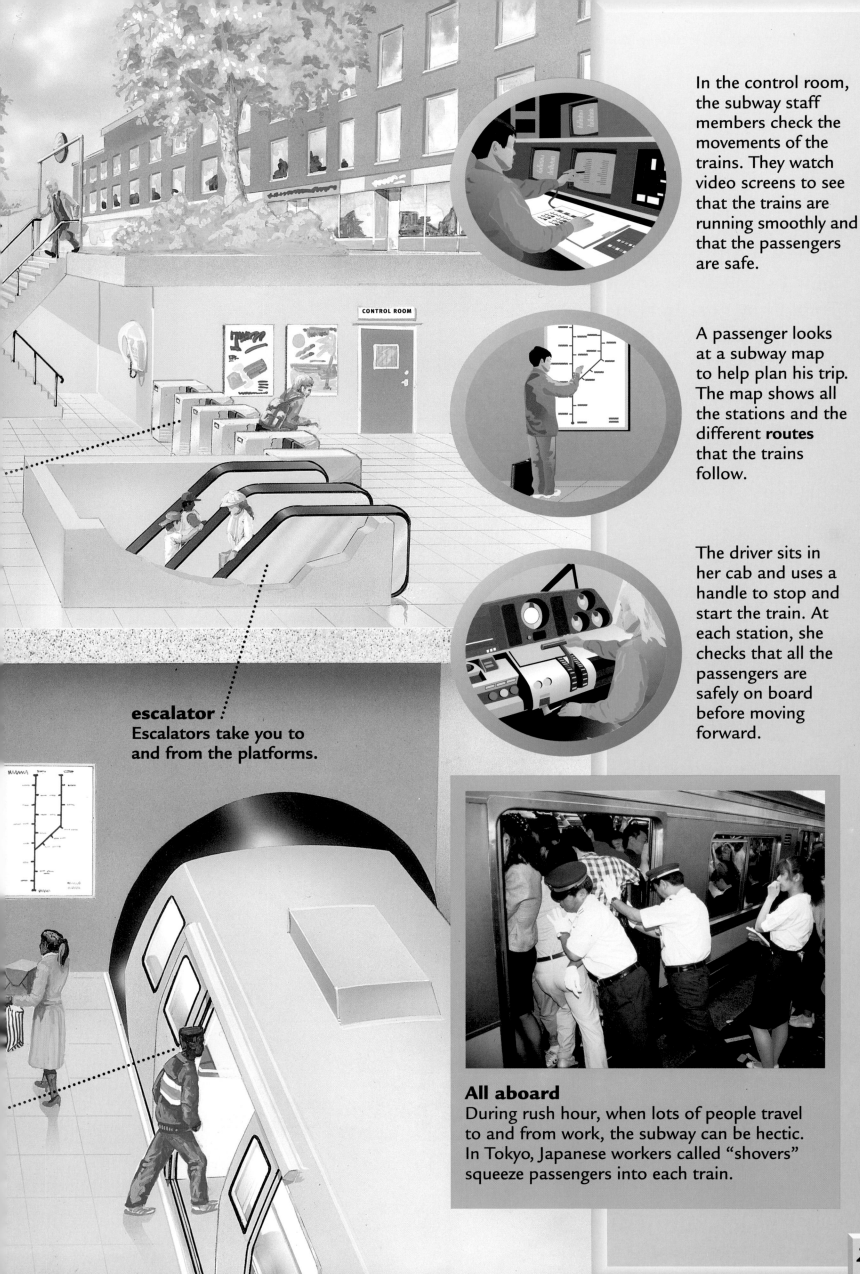

In the control room, the subway staff members check the movements of the trains. They watch video screens to see that the trains are running smoothly and that the passengers are safe.

A passenger looks at a subway map to help plan his trip. The map shows all the stations and the different **routes** that the trains follow.

The driver sits in her cab and uses a handle to stop and start the train. At each station, she checks that all the passengers are safely on board before moving forward.

CONTROL ROOM

escalator
Escalators take you to and from the platforms.

All aboard
During rush hour, when lots of people travel to and from work, the subway can be hectic. In Tokyo, Japanese workers called "shovers" squeeze passengers into each train.

Go to Ferry page 26, Harbor page 30, Working boats page 28

Traveling on water

Small boats were one of the first kinds of transportation to be invented. People powered these early boats by using their arms to move poles, paddles, and oars through the water. Later, they added sails so that the wind moved the boat along. Today, huge **cargo** ships and passenger liners, driven by massive **diesel engines**, sail back and forth across the oceans.

mast
The mast that holds up these sails is as high as a four-story house.

Reed boat
For thousands of years, people have used natural **materials** from their environment to build boats. On Lake Titicaca, in the mountains of South America, local people build fishing canoes from reeds that grow on the banks of the lake.

sail
Yacht sails are triangular with a curved outside edge.

Yacht
The tall sails of a modern yacht catch the wind and carry the boat across the waves. The clever sail design allows a yacht to move in any direction except straight into the wind. Large racing yachts compete in long ocean races, sometimes traveling all the way around the world.

crew
The crew members wear life jackets to keep them afloat in case they fall overboard in rough weather.

rudder
To help steer the boat, a crew member moves the rudder.

Ocean liner

Before the age of huge passenger airplanes, people sailed the seas on ocean liners. It took about four days to sail from London to New York, a journey that now takes seven hours by airplane. Today, liners are mostly used for vacation cruises. The body of an ocean liner is made of metal, which is heavier than water. It floats because the **hull** is full of air, which is lighter than the water around it.

Life on board

An ocean liner is a luxurious hotel on water. It has everything a passenger needs. On the sun **deck**, passengers relax beside the swimming pool. Afterward, they can play sports, visit restaurants, or see a movie before going to sleep in their comfortable cabins.

Speedboat

A speedboat skims lightly over the surface of the water at up to 40 mi. (65 km) per hour, which is almost as fast as a car on a highway. Speedboats are ideal for emergency rescue services, the coast guard, customs officers, and other people who need to travel quickly over short distances.

Houseboat

A houseboat is a floating home. In parts of Asia, where houseboats have been used for hundreds of years, many of them never leave their moorings. Modern houseboats are often fitted with powerful engines and used as vacation homes.

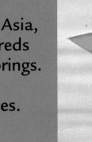

Go to Harbor page 30, Traveling on water page 24, Working boats page 28

Ferry

A ferry is a boat that transports people and **vehicles** across a stretch of water. Ferries operate in the same way as buses and trains, keeping to the same **routes** and times every day. Most ferries are huge boats that carry hundreds of passengers. During the voyage, passengers leave their cars and relax in lounges and restaurants.

▶This ferry travels across the sea. It is designed so that vehicles can drive onto the boat at one end and off the other.

radar mast
The **radar** lets the crew know how close other ships are and if land is nearby.

bridge
The captain controls the ferry and directs the crew from the bridge.

docking door
At the front and back, there are huge watertight doors. They swing open to allow vehicles to drive on and off.

propeller
At the front, spinning propellers help the boat to turn. At the back, more propellers drive it forward.

funnel
A funnel is like a giant chimney. It carries away smoke and fumes from the ship's **engines**.

lifeboat
In an emergency, passengers put on life jackets and are lowered into the water in a lifeboat.

passenger deck
On the passenger decks, people eat, relax, and visit the shops.

engine
This ferry has two **diesel** engines. They drive the propellers and provide **electricity** for heat and light.

stabilizer
In rough seas, stabilizers help keep the ship from rolling from side to side.

car deck
Vehicles are parked close together on the car **decks**.

Hovercraft
Some ferries, called hovercraft, float along on a cushion of air. Large fans suck the air through a funnel and into a giant rubber base that keeps the air in place. The hovercraft then speeds along just above the surface of the water.

Go to Harbor page 30, Traveling on water page 24, Underwater boats page 32

Working boats

Boats come in many shapes and sizes and each kind is designed to do a particular job. They may fight harbor fires or cut a path through frozen seas so that other boats can pass. The world's largest boats are tankers and container ships. They transport heavy **cargo**, including food, cars, and oil, across the ocean to countries on the other side of the world.

Container ship

In the past, goods were loaded onto a ship by hand, which could take up to a week. Today, a container ship can be loaded in less than 24 hours. Giant metal containers are filled with goods at a factory, then taken by truck or train to the harbor where a crane lowers them into place on the ship. Loading is easy because all the containers are the same size, and they can be stacked up like piles of huge bricks.

Supertanker

This supertanker carries oil that has been pumped into its hull through the long pipes on **deck**. Some supertankers are the largest ships ever built — they stretch the length of four football fields. Once they are moving, they take several miles to stop.

crane
Giant cranes lift up to 2,000 containers onto the ship.

hull
First, the containers are stacked inside the ship's hull. The extra containers are piled high on the deck.

Fishing trawler

A fishing trawler is designed to remain stable even in rough seas. The crew members use special **sonar** equipment to find groups of fish beneath the waves. Then they lower a net into the water to make their catch. When the fish are on board, they are stored in ice to keep them fresh until the trawler reaches land.

winch
The heavy net is cranked on board using a winch.

fishing net
This fishing net is called a trawl. Small holes in the net allow young fish to escape.

Fireboat

A fireboat waits in a harbor or on a city river in case a fire breaks out on other boats or in buildings close to the water's edge. They use powerful pumps to squirt jets of water or foam onto a fire to put it out. A fireboat also carries ladders, breathing equipment, and first-aid kits to help with rescues and to treat injuries.

Icebreaker

An icebreaker travels in front of other ships in icy seas or lakes. It has a powerful **engine** and an extra-strong hull that breaks up the ice ahead, clearing a path for the ships behind it. Powerful propellers at both the front and back help the boat to turn or reverse out of the ice.

Go to Ferry page 26, Traveling on water page 24, Working boats page 28

Harbor

A harbor is a calm, sheltered area of water where boats start or end their journeys. Most are natural shelters, where the land curves to make a bay or a wide river joins the sea. A few harbors, built by people, have high stone walls to keep out rough waves. At a large harbor, ships arrive daily to pick up **cargo** and drop off passengers.

▶ A busy harbor is full of all kinds of boats—from giant ferries to sailboats and motorboats.

lighthouse
A flashing lighthouse warns sailors that they are close to land.

buoy
Floating buoys mark a safe **route** through the water for boats.

dredger
A dredger clears mud from the harbor bottom so that the water remains deep enough for large boats.

marina
After a cruise, owners tie up their motorboats and yachts in the marina.

quay
The quay is a platform where boats are **moored**. A quay that stretches out across the water is called a pier.

30

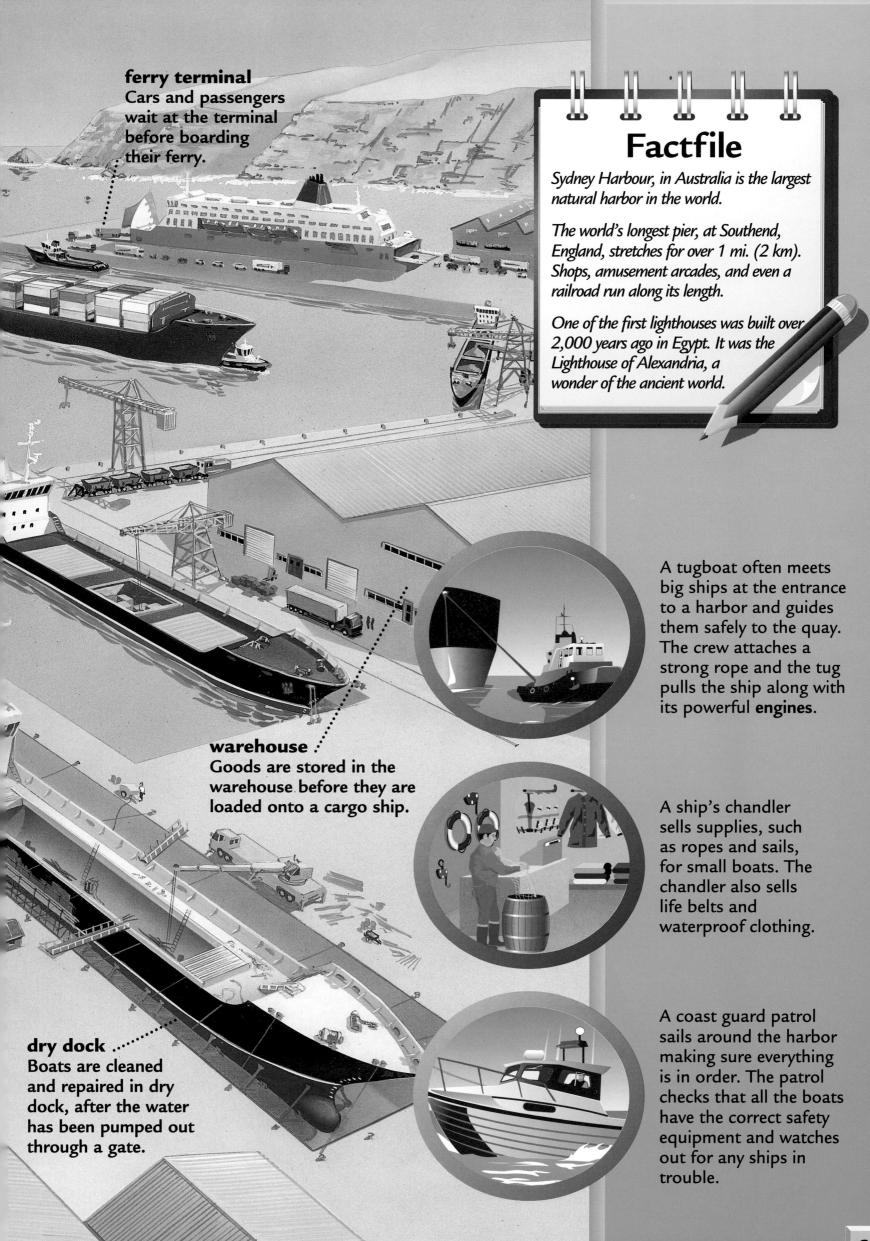

ferry terminal
Cars and passengers wait at the terminal before boarding their ferry.

Factfile

Sydney Harbour, in Australia is the largest natural harbor in the world.

The world's longest pier, at Southend, England, stretches for over 1 mi. (2 km). Shops, amusement arcades, and even a railroad run along its length.

One of the first lighthouses was built over 2,000 years ago in Egypt. It was the Lighthouse of Alexandria, a wonder of the ancient world.

A tugboat often meets big ships at the entrance to a harbor and guides them safely to the quay. The crew attaches a strong rope and the tug pulls the ship along with its powerful **engines**.

warehouse
Goods are stored in the warehouse before they are loaded onto a cargo ship.

A ship's chandler sells supplies, such as ropes and sails, for small boats. The chandler also sells life belts and waterproof clothing.

A coast guard patrol sails around the harbor making sure everything is in order. The patrol checks that all the boats have the correct safety equipment and watches out for any ships in trouble.

dry dock
Boats are cleaned and repaired in dry dock, after the water has been pumped out through a gate.

Underwater boats

Most boats float on top of the water, but a few kinds dive into the depths. There they do many jobs, from exploring the sea floor to searching for shipwrecks or repairing oil rigs. An underwater boat carries air for its crew to breathe. It must also be extremely strong to avoid being crushed by the **pressure**, or push, of the water around it.

▼ This underwater boat, called a **submersible**, is studying animals and plants on the sea floor.

sonar
Special **sonar** equipment warns of underwater obstacles, such as mountains or big rocks.

view port
The crew studies the sea floor through the glass view port.

video camera
In dark waters, a special video camera shows the crew what lies nearby.

robot arm
Robot arms collect samples from the sea floor. They are also useful for carrying out repairs.

sample basket
Samples are put into a basket and studied later.

cabin
Inside the cabin, there are controls for steering the submersible and working the robot arms.

Factfile

In 1985, a submersible discovered the wreck of the Titanic, *a luxury liner that sank during its first voyage in 1912.*

One of the first **submarines** was built over 300 years ago. Twelve men rowed it along the River Thames in England, breathing air through pipes that jutted above the surface of the water.

Underwater robots
This submersible is a Remote Operated Vehicle (ROV). It does not carry a crew and is controlled from a ship on the surface of the ocean.

propeller
A spinning propeller pushes the submersible along.

How a submarine dives
In war time, a submarine is used to find and attack enemy ships and submarines. It has ballast tanks that allow it to dive and surface.

Diving

air is let out

ballast tank

water rushes in

1 Air is let out of the ballast tanks and water rushes in. This makes the submarine heavier and it starts to dive.

Surfacing

air is pumped in

ballast tank

water is pushed out

2 Air is pumped into the ballast tanks, pushing the water out. The submarine becomes lighter and starts to rise.

ballast tanks
These tanks are filled with air or water to make the submersible move up or down.

Go to Airplane page 36, Airport page 40, Helicopter page 38

Traveling in the air

People have always dreamed of flying through the air, but nobody knew how until about 200 years ago. The earliest successful flights took place in hot-air balloons toward the end of the 1700's. In 1903, Orville Wright became the first person to fly a powered airplane. It was called *The Flyer* and flew just 120 ft. (37 m). Today, airplanes fly all over the world, carrying hundreds of passengers at a time.

Hot-air balloon

In 1783, Jacques and Joseph Montgolfier launched the first passengers in a hot-air balloon. They were a cockerel, a duck, and a pig! Today, people ride in balloons for fun. A roaring flame heats the air inside the balloon, making it lighter than the air around it. This makes the balloon rise, lifting the basket off the ground. When it is in the sky, the wind carries the balloon high across the ground.

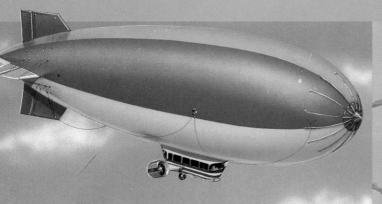

Airship

An airship is a balloon that has **engines** to drive it forward. The balloon contains a light gas called helium that allows it to float in the sky. The pilot, who steers the balloon, and a few passengers travel in the small cabin that hangs underneath. Often, airships hover above big sports events so that cameras in the cabin can film the action below.

Glider

A glider is similar to an airplane but it does not have an engine. To take off, an airplane tows the glider into the sky or a moving car pulls it up on a wire, like a kite, then lets it go. When the glider is in the air, the pilot looks for patches of rising air. The glider's narrow wings catch the rising air, lifting it higher.

Float plane

Most airplanes need a long runway to make a landing, but a float plane can land on a lake, a river, or on the sea. Instead of wheels, it has two large, canoelike floats that rest on the surface of the water and stop the plane from sinking. This float plane has traveled far out to sea to pick up divers who are carrying out underwater research.

Jump jet

This Harrier is called a jump **jet** or V/STOL (Vertical/Short Take-Off and Landing) because when it takes off, it **launches** straight up. On each side of the jet are nozzles. The powerful engine blasts air through these nozzles, pushing up the jet. Jump jets can fly forward, hover in one place, and go backward.

cockpit
The tiny cockpit is just big enough for the pilot who flies the jet.

nozzle
The nozzles swivel to change the direction in which the plane flies.

aircraft carrier
An aircraft carrier is a ship with a runway so that airplanes can take off at sea.

Space shuttle

A space shuttle can fly **astronauts** into space and back many times. Two **booster rockets** and three powerful engines blast the shuttle into space, where it travels around Earth. When the shuttle returns, it glides down to the runway without using any of its engines.

Airplane

A modern passenger airplane carries hundreds of people all over the world. It travels high above the clouds at more than 500 mi. (800 km) per hour. Outside the airplane, the air is freezing cold and too thin for people to breathe, but inside the cabin, the passengers can breathe normally. They relax, eat meals, watch films, and even make telephone calls as they speed across the world.

wing
The airplane's wings are curved on top. Their special shape helps the airplane to rise into the air.

flight deck
The captain and the copilots take off, fly, and land the airplane from the flight deck.

galley
In the galley, the cabin crew heats up meals for everyone on board. Trays of food are loaded before take-off.

nose
Inside the nose, there is a weather **radar** that warns the pilot when there is a storm ahead.

engine
This airplane is powered by four huge **jet engines**.

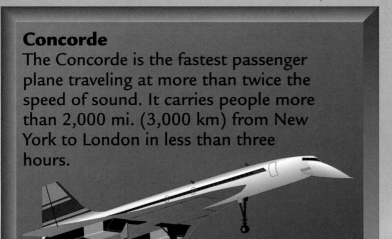

fin ....
The fin keeps the airplane in a straight line and stops it from rolling from side to side.

rudder
Moving the rudder helps the airplane turn left or right.

cabin
More than 300 passengers can fit into this cabin. For take-off, they sit upright and fasten their seat belts.

On the flight deck
The flight deck is filled with dials, switches, and computer screens showing all kinds of flight information. During take-off, the pilot watches his speed closely and checks that the runway ahead is clear.

wing flap
The wing flaps move up and down. This helps the airplane to lift up during take-off and to brake when it lands.

Go to Airplane page 36, Emergency vehicles page 18, Traveling in the air page 34

Helicopter

A helicopter is an aircraft with whirling **rotors** that allow it to fly. It cannot travel as fast as most airplanes but it moves easily, flying straight up and down, hovering in one spot, and even landing in tiny spaces, such as on top of a skyscraper. Helicopters do many different jobs, from reporting on traffic conditions to fighting fires and taking people to the hospital in an emergency.

▶ This helicopter is rescuing a climber who was stranded on a mountain.

control levers ....
By moving the control levers, the pilot can make the helicopter fly up and down or backward and forward.

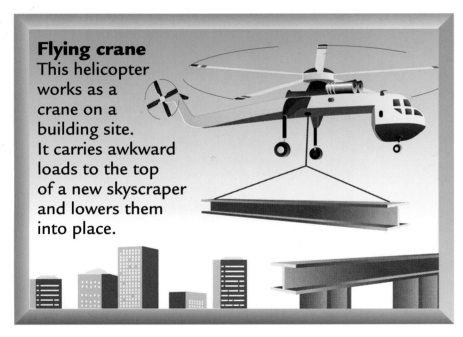

Flying crane
This helicopter works as a crane on a building site. It carries awkward loads to the top of a new skyscraper and lowers them into place.

Crop spraying
Some farmers use helicopters fitted with special equipment to spray their crops with fertilizer or spread seeds across a field.

Factfile

In 1483, the great artist and inventor Leonardo da Vinci designed a helicopter but he never built it.

The first helicopter that could fly was a model built in 1784. It had two feather rotors to lift it into the air.

In 1989, a helicopter hovered in one spot for over two days. This is the longest hover on record.

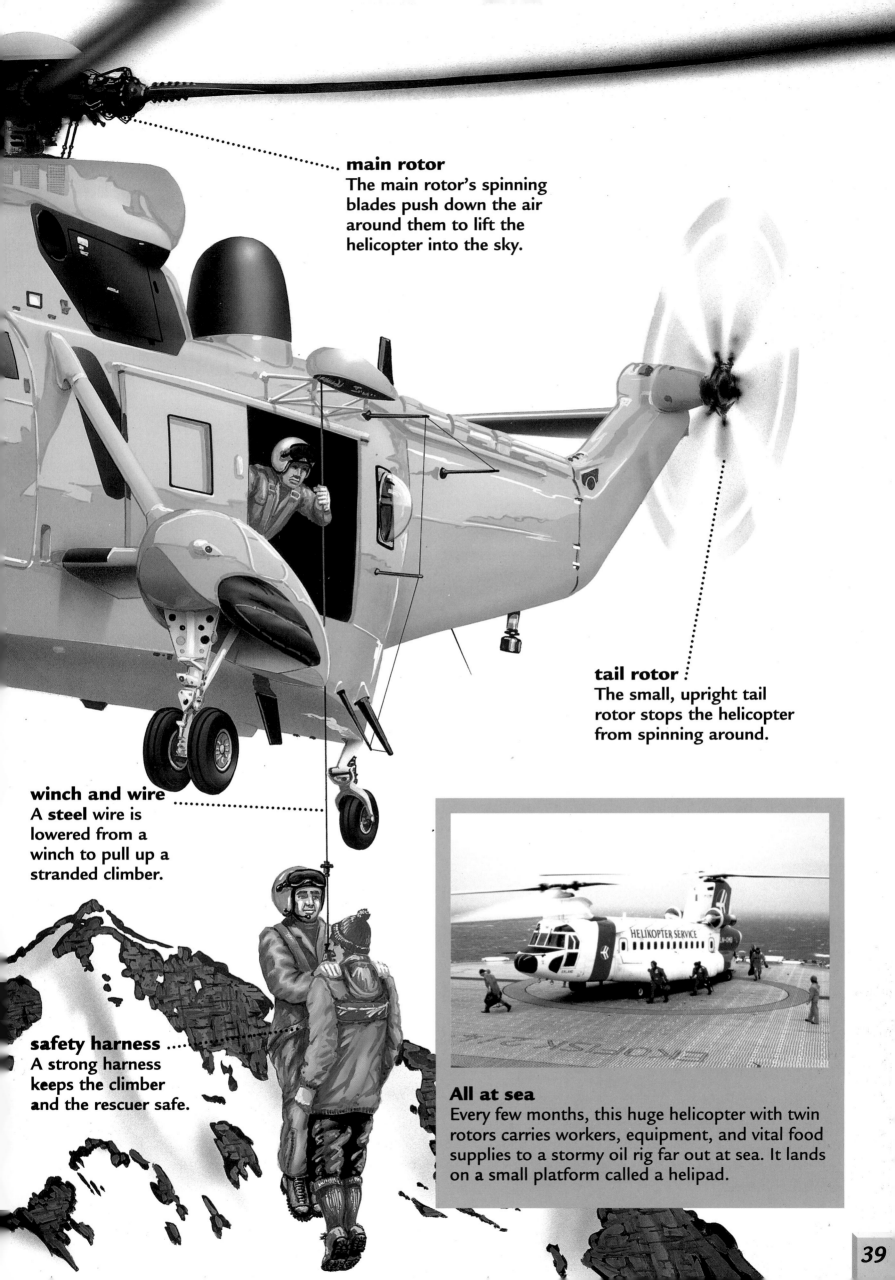

main rotor
The main rotor's spinning blades push down the air around them to lift the helicopter into the sky.

tail rotor
The small, upright tail rotor stops the helicopter from spinning around.

winch and wire
A **steel** wire is lowered from a winch to pull up a stranded climber.

safety harness
A strong harness keeps the climber and the rescuer safe.

All at sea
Every few months, this huge helicopter with twin rotors carries workers, equipment, and vital food supplies to a stormy oil rig far out at sea. It lands on a small platform called a helipad.

Go to Airplane page 36, Emergency vehicles page 18, Traveling in the air page 34

Airport

An international airport is as busy as a small city, with airplanes taking off and landing nonstop. Each day, thousands of passengers pass through a large airport and almost as many people work here, from air-traffic controllers and customs officers to restaurant staff. Everyone makes sure that the airport runs safely and smoothly.

▼ Teams of people are needed to prepare a plane for take-off.

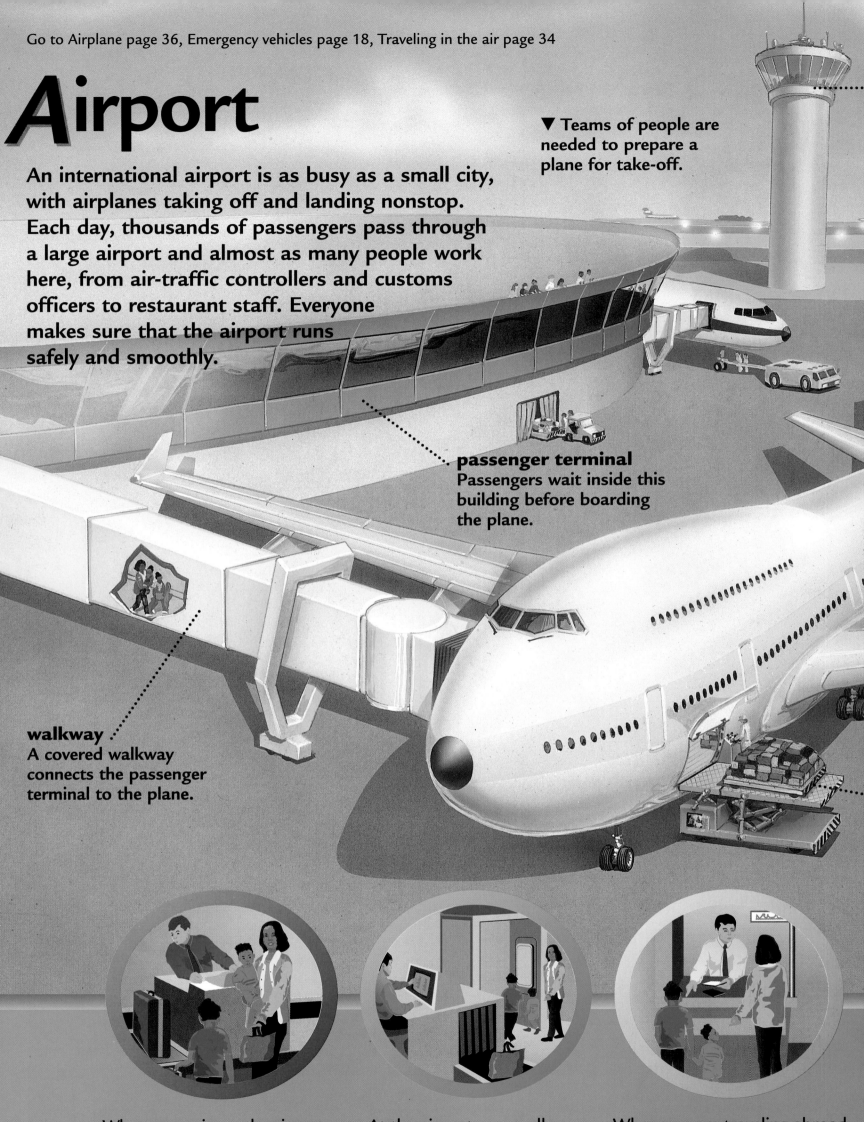

passenger terminal
Passengers wait inside this building before boarding the plane.

walkway
A covered walkway connects the passenger terminal to the plane.

When you arrive at the airport, you check in. An airline employee takes your heavy luggage for loading onto the plane and gives you a boarding pass.

At the airport, you walk through a security gate that makes sure that you are not carrying anything dangerous. An X-ray machine is used to look inside your bag.

When you are traveling abroad, you need to go to passport control. Here, an official makes sure that your passport is up to date.

control tower
From this tower, air-traffic controllers tell pilots when it is safe to take off and land.

runway
This runway is over 2 mi. (3 km) long. Bright lights clearly mark the runway in bad weather and at night.

airport bus
Buses carry people to planes parked far away from the passenger terminal.

emergency vehicles
Ambulances and fire engines are always ready in case of an emergency.

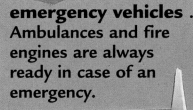

refueling tanker
A tanker fills giant tanks in the plane's wings with thousands of gallons of **fuel**.

cargo loader
A **cargo** loader lifts the passengers' heavy luggage into the **hold**.

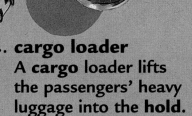

In the departure lounge, the overhead monitors tell you when your flight is ready to leave. There may be enough time for a snack.

Finally, you make your way to the boarding gate. Here, the air crew check your boarding pass before you board the plane. Enjoy your flight!

Factfile

One of the busiest airports in the world is O'Hare International Airport in Chicago. A plane takes off or lands there about every 90 seconds.

In Japan, an entire island had to be built, nearly 3 mi. (5 km) out to sea, to make enough space for Kansai International Airport. Roads link the airport to the mainland.

Go to Traveling in the air page 34

Traveling on snow

When heavy snow falls, **vehicles** with wheels are not much use. The wheels cannot grip the road properly, and they sink into the soft snow. People who live in the cold north and explorers often use special vehicles fitted with long, narrow skis instead of wheels. The skis slide smoothly along on top of the snow without sinking.

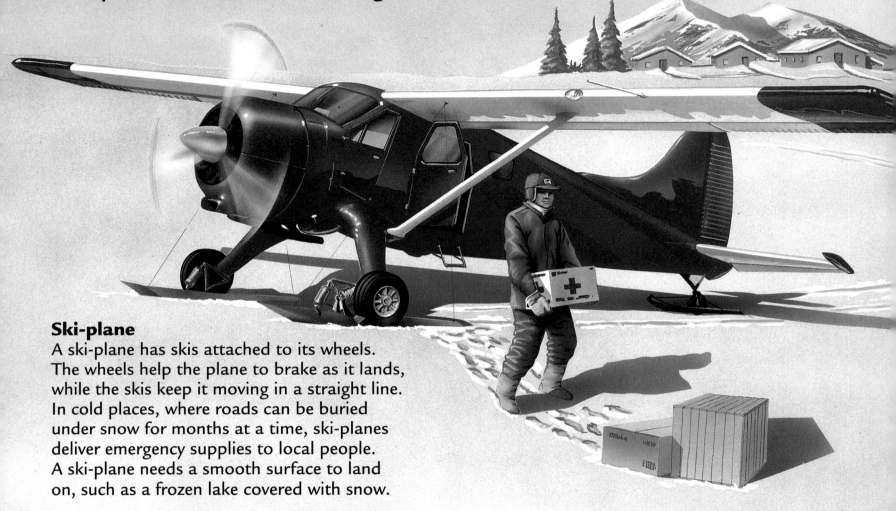

Ski-plane

A ski-plane has skis attached to its wheels. The wheels help the plane to brake as it lands, while the skis keep it moving in a straight line. In cold places, where roads can be buried under snow for months at a time, ski-planes deliver emergency supplies to local people. A ski-plane needs a smooth surface to land on, such as a frozen lake covered with snow.

Snowmobile

A snowmobile moves along on skis and **caterpillar tracks** instead of wheels. A small **engine** drives the tracks while the rider uses the handlebars to turn the skis left or right. Many people who live in the icy north travel by snowmobile because it is a quick way to get from place to place. They use their vehicles for hunting and fishing trips, for herding reindeer, and for rescuing people in an emergency.

42

Clearing the road

Clearing the road after a heavy snowfall, so that cars and trucks can pass by, is a job for a snowblower or a snowplow. The machine shown here is a snowblower. It scoops up the powdery snow in its huge curved blade and then blows it to one side of the road through a funnel. A snowplow is similar but instead of blowing the snow it pushes it away with a large blade that is set at an angle.

Skis and snowshoes

Walking across snow is difficult, so people wear skis and snowshoes to help them. In cold countries, many children travel to school on cross-country skis. Snowshoes strap onto the bottom of your boots to make walking much easier.

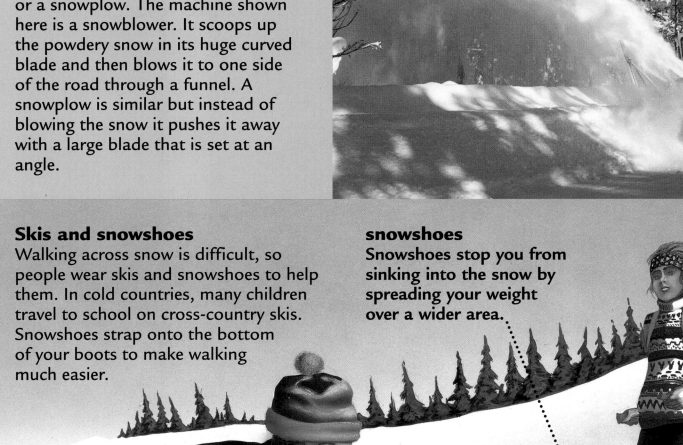

snowshoes
Snowshoes stop you from sinking into the snow by spreading your weight over a wider area.

skis
Cross-country skis are long and thin so that they slide along easily. They clamp onto the toes of your boots.

Reindeer sledge

For hundreds of years, sledges have carried people and heavy loads across the freezing snow. The sledges glide along on two curved runners. Teams of reindeer are pulling the sledges shown above but, in some places, a team of dogs, such as the Siberian husky, are often used.

Amazing facts

On these pages, you can discover amazing facts about all kinds of **vehicles**. You can learn about the biggest and fastest trucks, boats, and airplanes. You can also find out about strange inventions and what traveling may be like in the future.

How big is it?

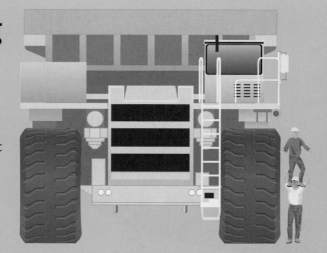

Wheely wonder
The Terex Titan is the world's biggest dump truck. Its giant tires are as tall as two people.

Amazing wings
The Spruce Goose had the longest wings of any airplane. They were longer than the Statue of Liberty is tall. It flew only once, in 1947.

Floating giant
The longest ship is the supertanker Jahre Viking. It is 1,503 ft. (458 m) long, which equals about 15 blue whales lined up end to end.

Strangest transport

People have invented several strange vehicles by mixing up all kinds of odd things!

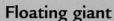

Pedal power
The Daedalus is a cross between a bicycle and an airplane. The pilot pushes the pedals to turn a propeller and move through the air.

Car in a suitcase
This experimental car fits inside a suitcase. When it is not being driven, the owner can fold it away and carry it.

Incredible journeys

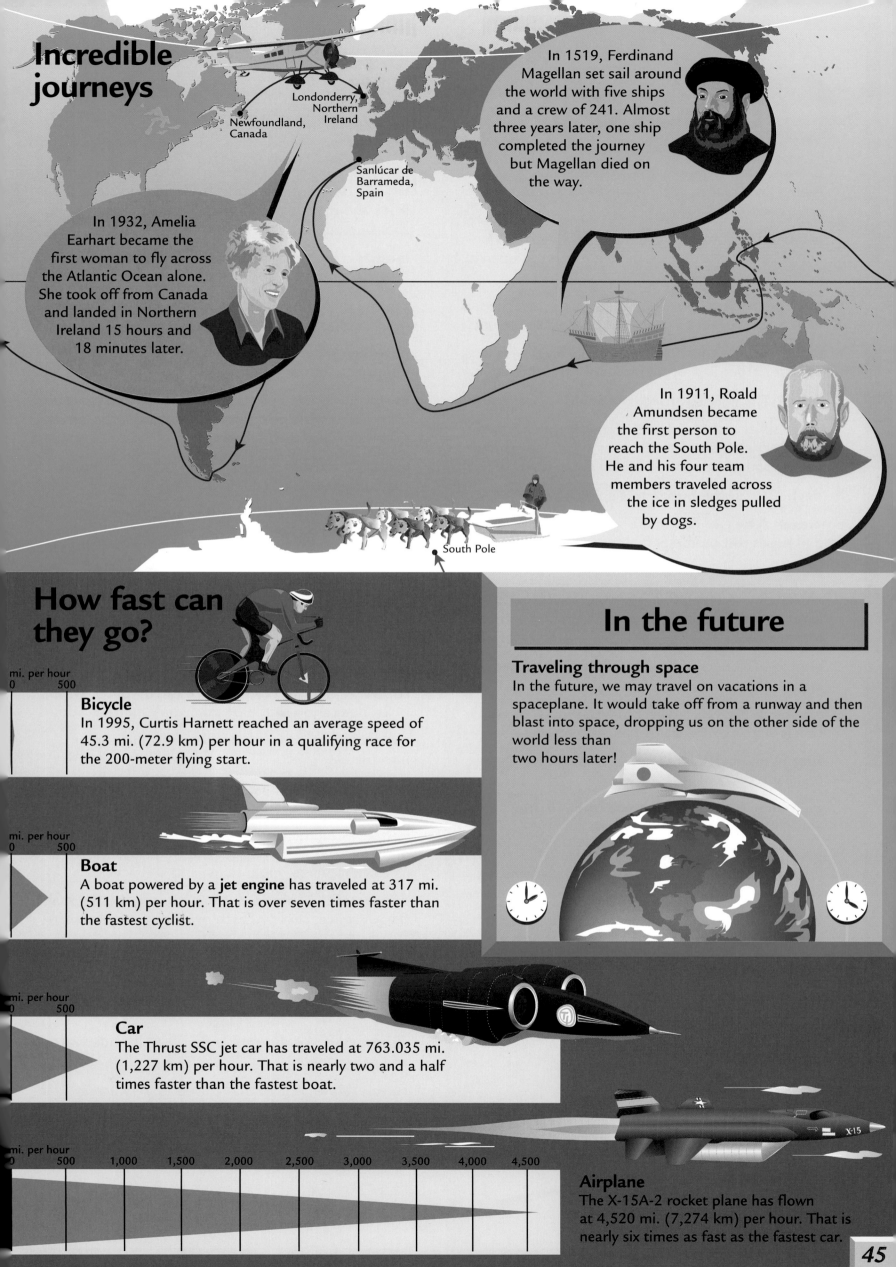

Londonderry, Northern Ireland

Newfoundland, Canada

Sanlúcar de Barrameda, Spain

In 1519, Ferdinand Magellan set sail around the world with five ships and a crew of 241. Almost three years later, one ship completed the journey but Magellan died on the way.

In 1932, Amelia Earhart became the first woman to fly across the Atlantic Ocean alone. She took off from Canada and landed in Northern Ireland 15 hours and 18 minutes later.

In 1911, Roald Amundsen became the first person to reach the South Pole. He and his four team members traveled across the ice in sledges pulled by dogs.

South Pole

How fast can they go?

mi. per hour
0   500

Bicycle
In 1995, Curtis Harnett reached an average speed of 45.3 mi. (72.9 km) per hour in a qualifying race for the 200-meter flying start.

mi. per hour
0   500

Boat
A boat powered by a **jet engine** has traveled at 317 mi. (511 km) per hour. That is over seven times faster than the fastest cyclist.

mi. per hour
0   500

Car
The Thrust SSC jet car has traveled at 763.035 mi. (1,227 km) per hour. That is nearly two and a half times faster than the fastest boat.

mi. per hour
0   500   1,000   1,500   2,000   2,500   3,000   3,500   4,000   4,500

Airplane
The X-15A-2 rocket plane has flown at 4,520 mi. (7,274 km) per hour. That is nearly six times as fast as the fastest car.

In the future

Traveling through space
In the future, we may travel on vacations in a spaceplane. It would take off from a runway and then blast into space, dropping us on the other side of the world less than two hours later!

Glossary

astronaut A person who travels into space to explore new places, such as the moon, or to carry out experiments.

automatic Something that works by itself. An automatic door does not need a person to open it. It opens by itself.

booster rocket A small rocket that is attached to a large space rocket to give extra power at take-off.

canal A large channel dug out and filled with water so that barges and other boats can travel along it.

cargo The goods carried by a **vehicle** such as a ship.

caterpillar track A band of metal plates linked together, which **vehicles** such as ditch diggers and snowmobiles use instead of wheels to travel off-road.

deck One of the floors on a ship or bus.

diesel A type of **fuel** made from oil. Most trucks and buses run on diesel fuel.

electric Powered by **electricity**.

electricity A type of energy that flows through wires to make **vehicles**, such as streetcars and some trains, work.

engine The part of a **vehicle** that gives power. The engine of a car burns **fuel** to make it move.

engineer A person who designs, builds, or repairs things such as **vehicles**, roads, and bridges.

fuel A **material** that burns in an **engine** to make it work.

gasoline A type of **fuel** made from oil. Most cars and motorcycles run on gasoline.

gears A set of special toothed wheels. Gears are used to change the speed at which a **vehicle's** wheels turn.

hold The large space inside an airplane or ship where luggage or goods are stored.

hull The main part of a ship or boat that sits in the water.

jet The name for an airplane powered by jet **engines**. A jet engine works by sucking in air at the front and mixing it with **fuel**. The mixture burns, shooting out hot **gases** at the back.

launch To lift off from the ground. A rocket is launched into space.

material A substance, such as metal, plastic, glass, or wood, from which an object is made.

moored When a ship is moored, it is tied up to a quay or to a floating buoy.

motor The part of a **vehicle** that uses **electricity** or burns **fuel** to make it move. Many trains have **electric** motors to turn their wheels.

muscles Parts inside your body, made of tough tissue, that shrink and relax to allow you to move.

pollute To give out or leave behind waste that damages the air, sea, or land.

pressure The push or force that an object feels when it is surrounded by water or gas, such as air.

radar Equipment that uses radio waves to spot objects out of view. Airplanes and ships use radar to spot mountains and storms, and other airplanes or ships.

robot A machine, controlled by a computer, which often does a job that a person would normally do.

rotor The spinning blades that lift a helicopter into the air.

route The path taken from one place to another. Buses follow the same route each day.

sonar Equipment that uses sound to track underwater objects out of view. Ships use sonar to track icebergs, mountains, and shipwrecks.

spacecraft A **vehicle**, such as a space shuttle, that flies in space, circling Earth or visiting other planets.

steel A strong metal made mostly of iron that is often used to make cars and ships.

streamlined Having a smooth shape that cuts easily through air or water.

submarine A submersible that travels underwater and carries people.

submersible A ship that travels underwater.

vehicle A machine for carrying people and goods. Bicycles, cars, trains, ships, and airplanes are all vehicles.

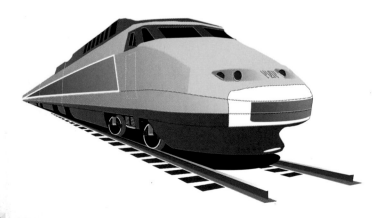

Index

Magellan, Ferdinand 45
maglev train 21
map 23
marina 30
mast 24, 26
mirror 9
Montgolfier, Joseph
  and Jacques 4, 34
moon 5, 11
Moscow 21
motor, electric 20
motorboat 30
motorcycle 8-9, 42
motor scooter 8
mountain bicycle 6
mountain rescue 38-39
muscle 6

Net, fishing 29
New York 21, 22, 25, 37
Northern Ireland 45
nozzle 35

Ocean liner 25, 33
off-ramp 14
oil 28
overpass 15
ox cart 4

Pallet 13
pannier 9
pantograph 17, 20
Paris 22
passenger 4, 10, 16, 20,
  21, 22, 23, 24, 25, 26,
  27, 30, 31, 34, 36, 37,
  40, 41
passenger terminal 40
passport 40
pedal of a bicycle 6
pier 30, 31
pilot 34, 35, 36, 37, 38,
  41, 44
police car 19
pollution 5, 6, 10, 17
power car 20
pressure 32
propeller 26, 27, 29,
  33, 44

Quay 30

Racing bike 7
radar 26, 36
radio 19, 20
railroad 12, 15, 20, 21,
  22, 23, 31
reed boat 24
reindeer 42, 43
Remote Operated Vehicle
  see ROV
rickshaw 7
road 7, 8, 12, 13, 14-15,
  16, 17, 41, 42, 43
road train 12
robot 11, 33
rocket 5, 35
rollerblades 7
rotor 38, 39
route 16, 23, 26, 30
ROV 33
rubber 6, 27
rudder 24, 37
runway 37, 41
Russia 5, 21

Safety cage 18
safety harness 39
sail 4, 24, 31
sailboat 4, 24, 30
school bus 17
Scotland 6
Seacat 27
seat belt 10, 38
ship see boat
shoulder 14
sign 14
siren 18
skateboarding 7
ski 42, 43
ski-plane 42
sled dog 43, 45
sledge 43, 45
sleeper 21
snow 42, 43
snowblower 43
snowmobile 42
snowplow 43
snowshoe 43
solar car 10
sonar 29, 32
South Pole 45
spacecraft 5, 35
spaceplane 45
space shuttle 5, 35
Spaghetti Junction 15
Spain 45
speedboat 25

Spruce Goose 44
stabilizer 27
station 16, 20, 21, 22, 23
steam train 4
steel 6, 17, 39
steering wheel 10
Stephenson, George 4
streamlining 7, 8
streetcar 16, 17
stretch limousine 11
submarine 33
submersible 32-33
subway 22-23
Sumerians 4
supertanker 28, 44
supporting jacks 18
Sydney Harbour 31

Tail rotor 39
tanker 28, 41
Terex Titan 44
Thames, River 33
Thrust SSC jet car 45
ticket machine 16, 22
tire 6, 7, 8, 13, 44
Titanic 33
Titicaca, Lake 24
Tokyo 23
tow truck 19
tractor 12
traffic jam 5, 7, 8, 10, 15
traffic light 14
trail bike 8
trailer 12
train 4, 20-23, 28
Trans-Siberian Railroad 21
trawler 29
tread 8
truck 12-13, 19, 43
trunk of a car 11
tug boat 31
tunnel 15, 22
turn signal 11
turntable 18

Underwater boat 32-33

Van 5

vehicle 5, 6, 9, 12, 14, 18,
  19, 26, 27, 41, 42, 44
Venice 27
video 23, 32
view port 32
Vinci, Leonardo da see
  Leonardo da Vinci
Vladivostok 21
Volkswagen Beetle 11
V/STOL 35

Walkway 40
warehouse 13, 31
water transport 4, 24-33,
  35, 44, 45
wheel 4, 6, 7, 8, 9, 10,
  11, 12, 21, 42
winch 29, 39
windshield 8
wing flap 37
wing mirror 9
wing of an airplane 34,
  36, 37, 44
working boat 28-29
Wright, Orville 5, 34
Wright, Wilbur 5

X-15A-2 rocket plane 45

Yacht 24, 30